I Know That!

Day and Night

Claire Llewellyn

W

FRANKLIN WATTS
LONDON • SYDNEY

First published in 2005 by Franklin Watts
96 Leonard Street, London EC2A 4XD

Franklin Watts Australia
Level 17/207 Kent Street, Sydney NSW 2000

Series adviser: Gill Matthews, non-fiction literacy
    consultant and Inset trainer
Series editor: Rachel Cooke
Editor: Sarah Ridley
Series design: Peter Scoulding
Designer: Jemima Lumley

Acknowledgements: Laurie Campbell/NHPA 13, 14 (box); Robert Canis/Frank Lane Picture Agency
4, 22l; Stephen Dalton/NHPA 21; Manfred Danegger/Still Pictures 9; Eye Ubiquitous/Hutchinson
16; Guy Edwards/WWI/Still Pictures 7b; Chris Fairclough imprint page, 7t, 10-11, 22r; Paal
Hermansen/NHPA 12; Derek Karp/NHPA 5; Steven Kazlowski/Still Pictures cover, 6; Ralph and
Daphne Keller/NHPA 20; Robin Scagell/Galaxy Picture Library 14-15, 23l; Steve Shott title page,
18, 19, 23r; Rod Smith/Ecoscene 17; Dave Watts/NHPA 8. Thanks to our models: Danny, Harry,
Jemma, Joe, Liam and Milly. Thanks also to Sheena Lasko and Slade Green Infant School.

A CIP catalogue record for this book is available from the British Library.
Dewey decimal classification number: 529'.1

ISBN: 0 7496 6368 5

Printed in Malaysia

Contents

It is morning

In the morning, the Sun rises.
We wake and begin a new day.

▲ *At sunrise, the sky begins to brighten.*

Some animals wake early in the morning.

Think about summer and winter mornings. In what ways are they different?

The Sun

All day the Sun gives us light.

▲ *During the morning, the Sun slowly climbs in the sky.*

By midday, the Sun is high above us.

The Sun is always there, even on cloudy days.

In the afternoon, the Sun sinks down again.

Light for life

Sunlight is important for plants and animals.

►*Plants need light to grow.*

▲ *Many animals need light to find their food.*

Our eyes need light to see. Can you think of three ways your sight helps you?

A busy day

Most of us are busy during the day.

▲ *Children go to school in the daytime.*

◀ We meet our friends at the park after school.

▶ Many people work during the day.

Which is your favourite part of the day? Why?

The end of the day

In the evening, the Sun sets.
The light begins to fade.

The sky grows dark at the end of the day.

▶ Birds look for a place to roost at night.

Think about summer and winter evenings. In what ways are they different?

Night-time

At night the sky is dark. It is cooler at night than during the day.

Try looking at the Moon through binoculars. What can you see?

▶ *On clear nights we can see the Moon and stars.*

In the dark

When it gets dark we cannot see.
We need to use lights then.

◀ People put on electric lights at home.

▲ *Drivers use headlights to see the road.*

Have you ever used a torch at
night? Where were you?

Fast asleep

We get tired by the end of the day. We go to bed and sleep.

▶ *Our bodies slow down at the end of the day.*

▼ *Sleeping is very good for our body.*

Some people work at night. What sort of jobs do you think they do?

19

Animals at night

Some animals sleep in the day. They come out to feed at night.

▶ *A possum's big eyes help it to see in the dark.*

Bats hunt for food at night. This bat is about to catch a moth.

Animals that are active at night are called 'nocturnal'.

I know that...

1 In the morning, the Sun rises.

2 The Sun gives us light during the day.

3 Sunlight helps plants to grow and animals to find food.

4 We are busy in the daytime.

5 In the evening, the Sun sets.

6 The sky is dark at night.

7 At night we need lights to help us see.

8 Most of us sleep at night.

9 Some animals come out to feed at night.

Index

About this book

I Know That! is designed to introduce children to the process of gathering information and using reference books, one of the key skills needed to begin more formal learning at school. For this reason, each book's structure reflects the information books children will use later in their learning career – with key information in the main text and additional facts and ideas in the captions. The panels give an opportunity for further activities, ideas or discussions. The contents page and index are helpful reference guides.

The language is carefully chosen to be accessible to children just beginning to read. Illustrations support the text but also give information in their own right; active consideration and discussion of images is another key referencing skill. The main aim of the series is to build confidence – showing children how much they already know and giving them the ability to gather new information for themselves. With this in mind, the *I know that...* section at the end of the book is a simple way for children to revisit what they already know as well as what they have learnt from reading the book.